This book is
dedicated to all children,
but especially those
who are critically ill
and fighting the fight
of their life.

Other Bestmann/Bunnell books:
"Where Does God Sleep, Momma?"

Printed and Bound in the U.S.A.

International Standard Book Number: 0-89900-665-5

Plant Your Dreams, My Child

written by
Nancy Bestmann

illustrated by
Gini Bunnell

Plant your dreams, my child—

Make this your special day.

Take all the gifts God gives you

as you go along your way.

Add
Faith and Hope
and Love
to all
you
say
and do–

Treat others with respect

as they will then treat you.

And never
stop
to worry
about
tomorrow's
day.

God's there with open arms—

To help you find your way.

He's promised
He will stay
close by—

His love is
bigger than
the sky—

So deep—
So wide—

So long—
So high—
So. . .

Plant your dreams and they will grow—

For you're a child of God, you know.